He was feeling very spunky the day he made them!

Don made these footprints when he was two weeks old.

Raising Don

The True Story of a Spunky Baby Tapir

by Georgeanne Irvine

San Diego Zoo
Wildlife Alliance
Press

Raising Don: The True Story of a Spunky Baby Tapir was published by San Diego Zoo Wildlife Alliance Press in association with Blue Sneaker Press. Through these publishing efforts, we seek to inspire children and adults to care about wildlife, the natural world, and conservation.

San Diego Zoo Wildlife Alliance is a nonprofit conservation organization that is committed to saving species worldwide by uniting its expertise in animal care and conservation science with its dedication to inspiring a passion for nature. Its vision is a world where all life thrives.

Paul Baribault, President and Chief Executive Officer
Shawn Dixon, Chief Operating Officer
David Miller, Chief Marketing Officer
Georgeanne Irvine, Director of Publishing
San Diego Zoo Wildlife Alliance
P.O. Box 120551
San Diego, CA 92112-0551
sdzwa.org | 619-231-1515

San Diego Zoo Wildlife Alliance's publishing partner is Blue Sneaker Press, an imprint of Southwestern Publishing House, Inc., 2451 Atrium Way, Nashville, TN 37214. Southwestern Publishing House is a wholly owned subsidiary of Southwestern Family of Companies, Nashville, Tennessee.

Christopher G. Capen, President, Southwestern Publishing House
Carrie Hasler, Publisher, Blue Sneaker Press
Kristin Connelly, Managing Editor
Lori Sandstrom, Art Director/Graphic Designer
swpublishinghouse.com | 800-358-0560

ISBN: 978-1-943198-14-6
Library of Congress Control Number: 2020947710
Printed in the Republic of Korea
10 9 8 7 6 5 4 3 2 1

To **spunky Don** the tapir,
who has touched my heart and
brought joy to so many people.

Acknowledgments

**MY DEEPEST GRATITUDE TO THE MANY PEOPLE WHO HELPED ME
SHARE DON'S UPLIFTING STORY WITH CHILDREN EVERYWHERE:**

Matt Akel; Kimberly Hyde; Janet Hawes; Becky Kier; Julie Anderson; Tina Silva; Tammy Batson;
Steve Hebert; Mike Langridge; Kim Weibel; Mary Dural; Joanne Mills; Ann Dahl Alfama; Robbie Clark;
Harold Steyns; Vil Chanthavisouk; Chelsea Lee, Nashville Zoo; Carmi Penny; Lisa Bissi; Jen MacEwen;
Ken Bohn; Tammy Spratt; Kim Turner; Matt Marinkovich, DVM; Mary-Ellen Jordan; Shelley Weiss;
Helene Hoffman; Carrie Hasler; Lori Sandstrom; Mary Sekulovich; Debra Erickson; Angel Chambosse;
Yvonne Miles; and Patricia Medici, Lowland Tapir Conservation Initiative.

Waiting for a Tapir Tot!

The wildlife care team at the San Diego Zoo thought for sure this was the day that Luna, a Baird's tapir, would have her baby. She was restless and seemed uncomfortable. The excited team waited and watched live video feeds of Luna on their phones and computers, but nothing happened—there was no baby. A few more days passed but there was still no baby.

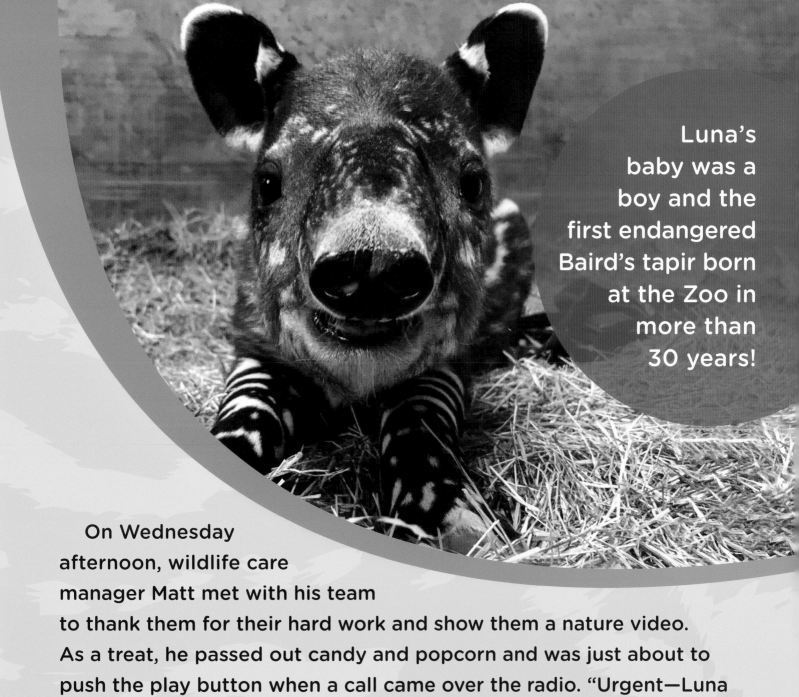

Luna's baby was a boy and the first endangered Baird's tapir born at the Zoo in more than 30 years!

On Wednesday afternoon, wildlife care manager Matt met with his team to thank them for their hard work and show them a nature video. As a treat, he passed out candy and popcorn and was just about to push the play button when a call came over the radio. "Urgent—Luna just gave birth!" exclaimed lead wildlife care specialist Tammy, who was checking on Luna before the meeting. Luckily, Tammy was there at just the right moment.

Baby tapirs are born with spots and stripes.

Matt and the wildlife care team raced to Luna's maternity area. On arriving, they could tell by the look on Tammy's face that something was wrong. Right after Luna gave birth, she was unsure of how to care for the baby, so she pushed him around. To keep the calf safe, Tammy quickly separated Luna from her newborn son. Zoo veterinarians arrived to make sure the calf was okay. The tiny tapir had a scrape on his shoulder but was fine otherwise.

When the wildlife care specialists tried to reintroduce Luna to her baby with a "howdy door" between them, she wasn't interested. Scientists don't know why a tapir mom might not care for her calf. But the Zoo's tapir experts guessed that because Luna was a first-time mom, maybe she was surprised by his birth and was now hesitant to be near him.

One thing was clear: the calf was hungry so a wildlife care specialist fed him his first bottle, which he finished right away.

A howdy door is a barrier between two animals so they can see, smell, and hear each other but can't touch.

Mama's Milk for Baby

Luna was reintroduced to her calf several more times, but she still didn't want him near her! Now the wildlife care specialists would need to raise and bottle-feed the little tapir. They knew it was best for him to drink his mother's milk, especially during his first days of life. Luna's milk would help protect the calf from diseases, so the caregivers came up with a plan: they would try to milk Luna just like they would milk a cow to provide some of her milk for the baby.

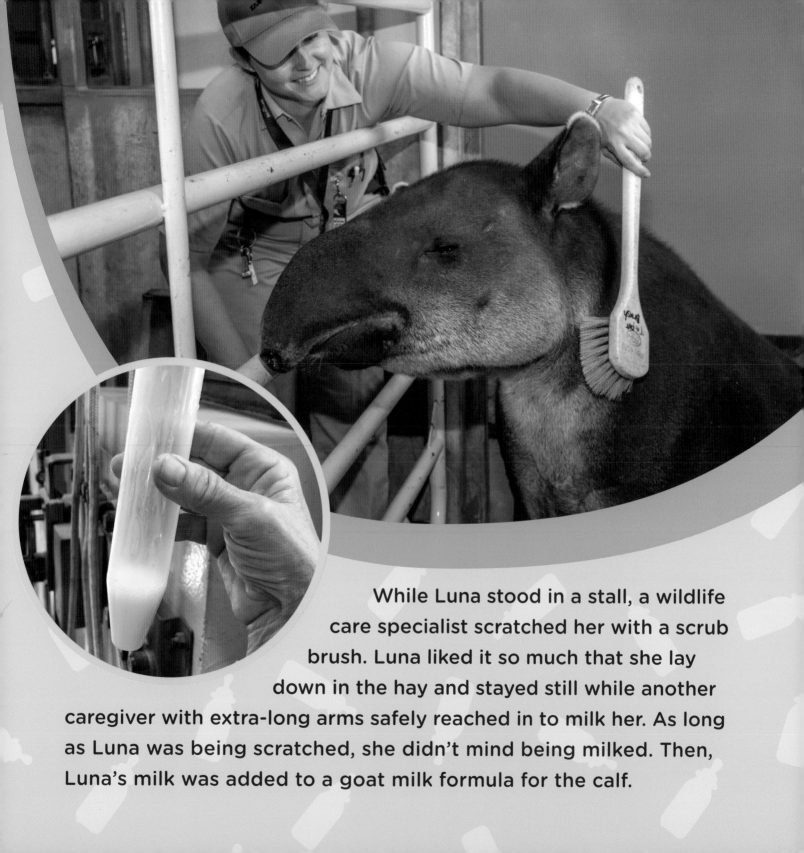

While Luna stood in a stall, a wildlife care specialist scratched her with a scrub brush. Luna liked it so much that she lay down in the hay and stayed still while another caregiver with extra-long arms safely reached in to milk her. As long as Luna was being scratched, she didn't mind being milked. Then, Luna's milk was added to a goat milk formula for the calf.

A Cute Watermelon with Legs

The baby tapir was named Don in honor of a Zoo veterinarian who had recently retired. Don quickly won the hearts of his caregivers—they loved his spunky, playful personality. They called him "the cutest watermelon in the world," because his stripes and spots made him look like a brown watermelon with legs.

Wildlife care specialist Becky often fed Don, who greeted her with a little chirp every time she arrived with his milk bottle. Don was a good eater but, he always wanted his back scratched and his face rubbed before he would take his bottle.

For Don's first few minutes of feeding, he stood up while Becky held the bottle. Then, he sat down to eat, similar to how a dog would sit. Don often finished his milk while lying down. That made it easy for Becky to rub his belly, which he expected after each meal.

Don was fed five times a day when he was little. Of course, he always wanted more when the bottle was empty!

A Tiny Tapir Trunk and Tiny Teeth

Don's nose was similar to an elephant's trunk, only shorter. He used it for smelling as well as picking up things like branches and bits of lettuce. The caregivers always smiled when Don lifted his mini trunk to sniff something because they could see his tiny tapir teeth that were beginning to grow.

After Don finished eating, he often grabbed the bottle with his tiny trunk and tried to run off with it! He liked playing, romping around in his pen, and exploring new areas—Don was curious about everything.

Don was fed small pieces of lettuce to start getting him used to veggies and leaves, which adult tapirs eat.

The wildlife care specialists kept daily records about Don's growth and activities. Some of the things they wrote down included how much milk he drank, his weight, which toys he played with, and whether or not he pooped. Keeping track of his poop helped them monitor his health.

Pool Party for Don

When Don was a week old, he was introduced to a shallow pool. All tapirs like to hang out near water and swim, which they learn from their mothers. Since Don's mom wasn't raising him, his caregivers became his swimming teachers.

Don liked to put his face in the water and blow bubbles with his nose and mouth.

At first, they had to coax, or gently urge, him into the water. Don had a tough time climbing into the pool because the sides were high and his front legs were short. He learned quickly, though, and was soon running, jumping, and belly flopping into the pool.

Tapirs also use ponds and pools as their potty, so the wildlife care specialists kept a close eye on Don's pool to make sure the water was clean.

A mother tapir gradually introduces her calf to the water, coaxing it to wade and swim.

Don was two weeks old when his caregivers introduced him to a pond in the habitat where the grown-up tapirs live with guanacos, capybaras, and a llama. Eventually, Don would live there too, but first he needed to feel comfortable in the pond, which was larger and deeper than his kiddie pool.

On Don's first day at the pond, it was filled with only three inches of water. The other animals were in a different area so they wouldn't bother or scare him—he would meet them later. Wildlife care specialist Kimberly tried to coax Don to the edge of a rocky ramp that led down to the water. He was curious but cautious and just sniffed at the rocks. The next day, Don walked partway down the ramp, even though it was steep, and Kimberly rewarded him with a back scratch.

Tapirs are related to horses and rhinos.

Each day that Don visited the pond, he got braver and braver. When he finally made it to the water's edge, Kimberly gently encouraged him, and then he took his first steps in.

As Don became more comfortable, Kimberly increased the depth of the water. She wore waders so she could stay close to him during his swimming lessons. Within a week, Don was walking in water up to his neck.

The little tapir grew more confident. His chirps and squeaks let Kimberly know he liked being in the deeper water.

Don would dog-paddle across the pond into the deep water.

Within a month of Don's first trip to the pond, he surprised Kimberly by dunking his head and swimming underwater for the first time. Of course, Don liked the extra back scratches and belly rubs he received for being such a good swimmer.

Making Friends

When Don began his swimming lessons, his only encounters with the other animals were through a fence. Now it was time to start meeting them.

The wildlife care specialists were concerned that some of the animals might bully Don. They wanted his first friend to be the sweetest animal in the habitat. The choice was easy: Bristle the capybara. She was the smallest of her litter, and when her mother died, the other capybaras picked on her. Even so, Bristle remained calm and friendly.

Capybaras are the world's largest rodents. They live in the wetlands of South America.

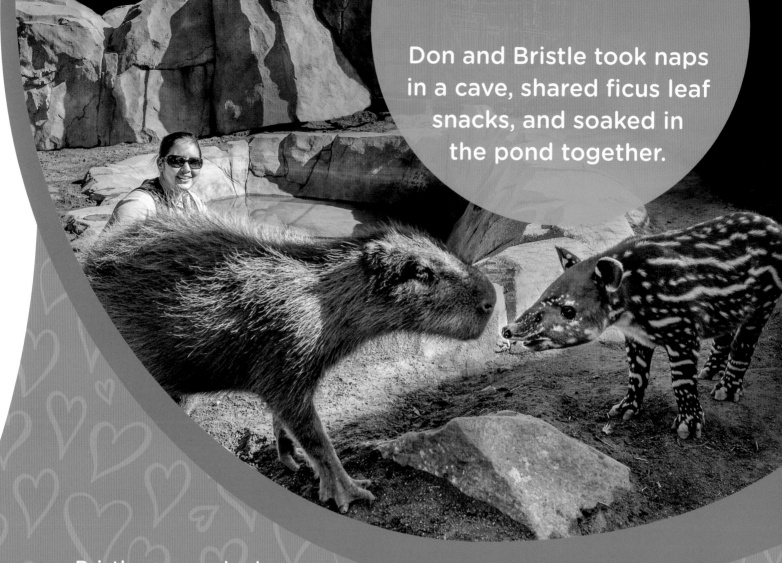

Don and Bristle took naps in a cave, shared ficus leaf snacks, and soaked in the pond together.

Bristle approached Don the first time they met. After they sniffed each other, they slowly became buddies.

A few days later, Don met the other capybaras, but they didn't like him and weren't very friendly to him. The wildlife care specialists decided Don should only spend time with Bristle for now. He could meet the other capybaras again when he was older and bigger.

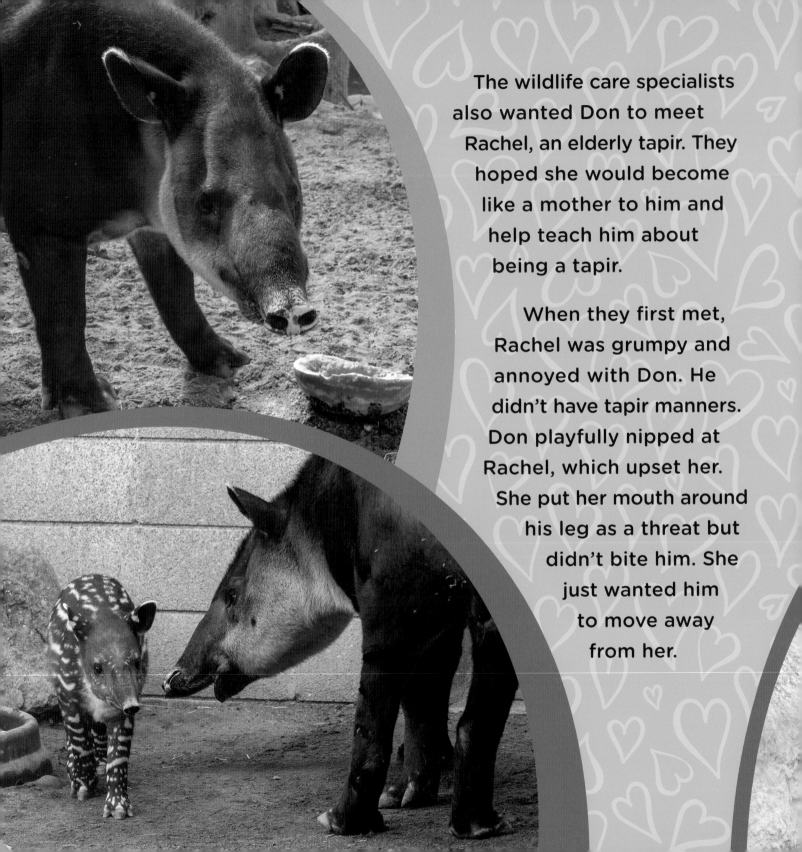

The wildlife care specialists also wanted Don to meet Rachel, an elderly tapir. They hoped she would become like a mother to him and help teach him about being a tapir.

When they first met, Rachel was grumpy and annoyed with Don. He didn't have tapir manners. Don playfully nipped at Rachel, which upset her. She put her mouth around his leg as a threat but didn't bite him. She just wanted him to move away from her.

At first, the wildlife care specialists supervised Don and Rachel whenever they were together. As Don got older, Rachel was friendlier to him because he was calmer and more mature. They even ate ficus leaves together. And once, when the caregivers put coconut oil on Don's back because his skin was dry, Rachel licked it off him. She liked the way it tasted!

Rachel was annoyed with Don's spunkiness.

But the guanacos and the llama didn't like Don at all. The guanacos first saw Don through a fence when he was a few days old. They sounded their alarm call, which is like a cross between a bleat and a laugh. Their ears were pinned back against their heads and they huffed and snorted at him.

Guanacos

Guanacos and llamas are related to camels.

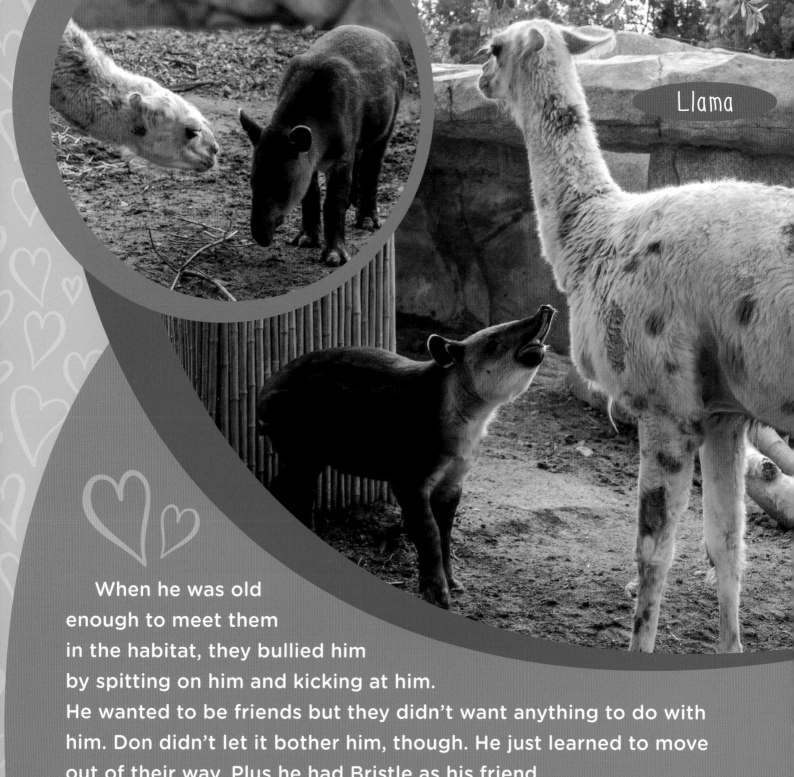

Llama

When he was old
enough to meet them
in the habitat, they bullied him
by spitting on him and kicking at him.
He wanted to be friends but they didn't want anything to do with
him. Don didn't let it bother him, though. He just learned to move
out of their way. Plus he had Bristle as his friend.

When Don was three months old, he weighed 121 pounds. He still drank milk formula from a bottle, but he also ate leaves, vegetables, and some fruits, including watermelon and bananas. He liked cucumbers and yams, but he wasn't fond of spinach, broccoli, or eggplant, although sometimes he ate them anyway.

After meals,
the wildlife care specialists
rubbed and lifted Don's feet so
when he grew up, he wouldn't mind having them touched or
examined. Tapirs have sensitive feet and need them looked at every
day to make sure there aren't any cuts, scrapes, or bruises. If Don
heard his caregivers cleaning the indoor area, he often banged on
the door, looking for a treat or rubdown.

Don was more confident now that he was older and bigger. He
even visited Rachel the tapir when she napped in the cave. Don often
used his big outdoor habitat as a racetrack—running as fast as he
could, spinning around, and then leaping into the pond.

No More Stripes and Spots

Don looked like a mini adult tapir by the time he was eight months old: his coat was still fuzzy but his stripes and spots were gone! He was energetic and rowdy but also friendly and gentle. Don lived with Rachel and Bristle as well as an older male tapir named Tatum, the rest of the capybaras, and sometimes the guanacos and the llama. Bristle was still his best friend, though.

For his first birthday, Don received an extra serving of his favorite vegetables and fruits. Then he went for a swim in the pond.

In a few more months, Don would be leaving the San Diego Zoo to live at the Nashville Zoo in Tennessee. There, he would meet a female tapir and hopefully become a father someday.

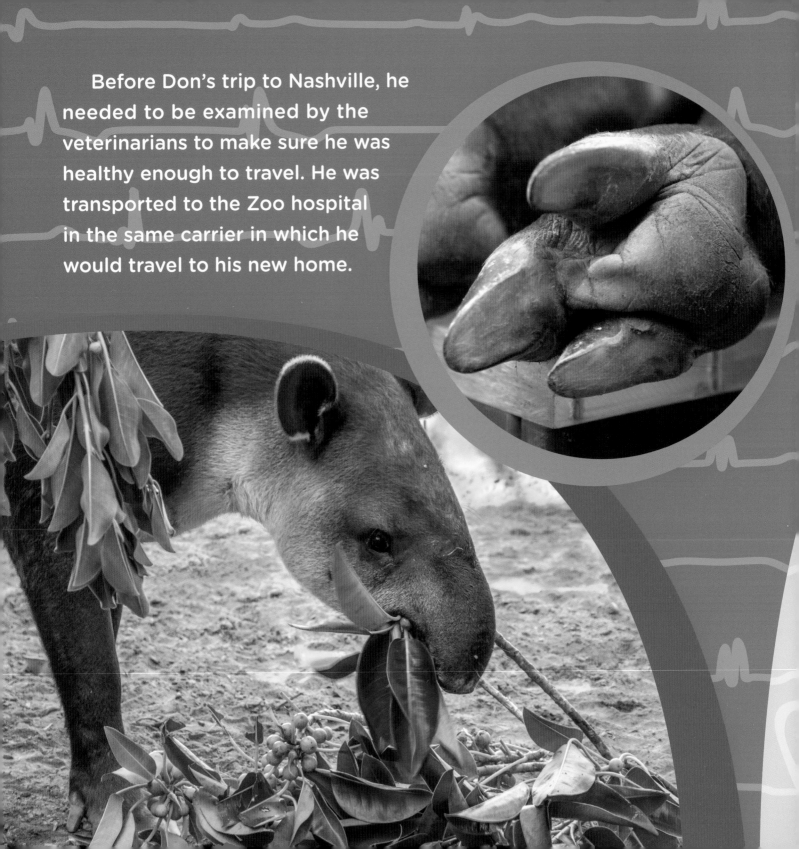

Before Don's trip to Nashville, he needed to be examined by the veterinarians to make sure he was healthy enough to travel. He was transported to the Zoo hospital in the same carrier in which he would travel to his new home.

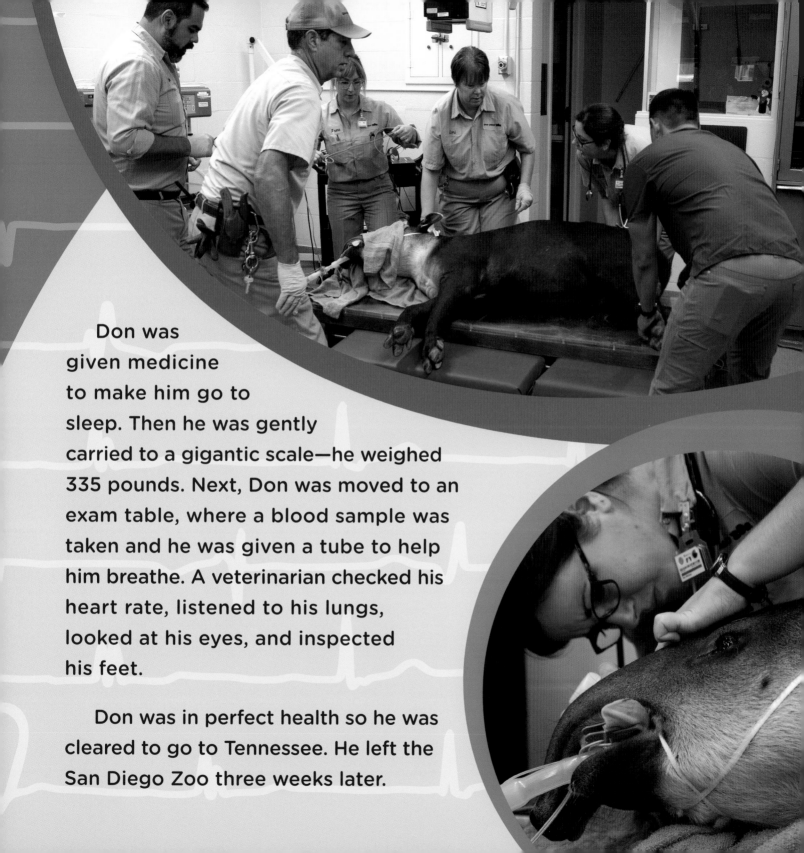

Don was given medicine to make him go to sleep. Then he was gently carried to a gigantic scale—he weighed 335 pounds. Next, Don was moved to an exam table, where a blood sample was taken and he was given a tube to help him breathe. A veterinarian checked his heart rate, listened to his lungs, looked at his eyes, and inspected his feet.

Don was in perfect health so he was cleared to go to Tennessee. He left the San Diego Zoo three weeks later.

Shortly after Don arrived in Nashville, his mother Luna gave birth to another calf— a daughter named Taiyari. The wildlife care specialists at the San Diego Zoo were overjoyed because this time, Luna was taking care of her baby!

Although Luna didn't raise Don, his dedicated caregivers made sure he had the best life possible. They helped him overcome the challenge of not being cared for by his mother. And, while Don was bullied when he was little, he grew up to be a confident adult who gets along with other animals.

Taiyari means "our heart" in the language of Mexico's Huichol people.

Juju

Now Don lives in a spacious habitat in the rolling hills of Tennessee. He has won the hearts of his new caregivers with his spunky attitude. Don has a pond for swimming, tall trees so he can nap in the shade, and a new best friend—Juju, a female tapir. Best of all, someday in the near future, Don and Juju will become parents of their own precious calf, helping to bring more of these endangered animals into the world.

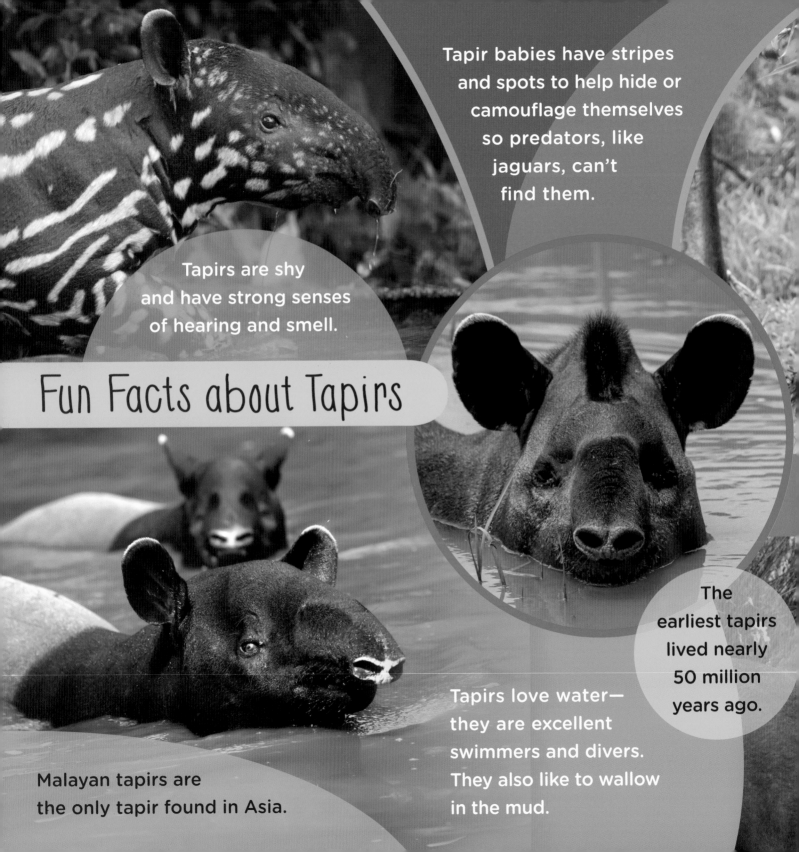

Tapir babies have stripes and spots to help hide or camouflage themselves so predators, like jaguars, can't find them.

Tapirs are shy and have strong senses of hearing and smell.

Fun Facts about Tapirs

The earliest tapirs lived nearly 50 million years ago.

Malayan tapirs are the only tapir found in Asia.

Tapirs love water—they are excellent swimmers and divers. They also like to wallow in the mud.

Tapirs make sounds that include high-pitched whistles, huffs, snorts, hiccups, and chirps.

A tapir's poop includes lots of seeds, which grow into new plants in the forest.

The name tapir comes from the word that Brazil's Tupi Indians called the animal: "tapyra."

In the wild, an adult tapir can eat up to 85 pounds of plants and fruits in one evening.

Adult tapirs weigh from 300 to 800 pounds, depending on the species.

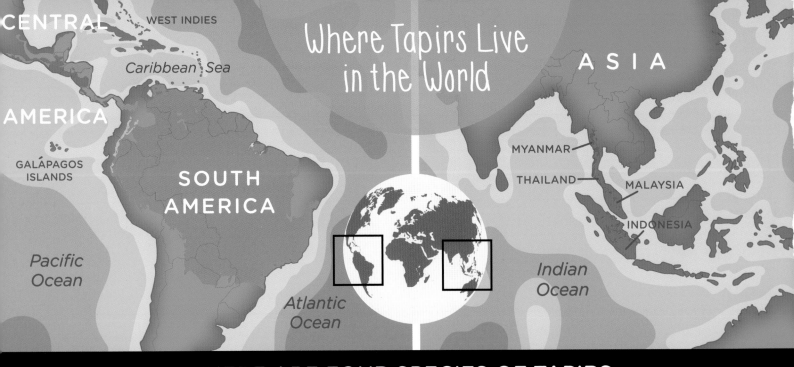

Where Tapirs Live in the World

CENTRAL
WEST INDIES
Caribbean Sea
AMERICA
GALÁPAGOS ISLANDS
SOUTH AMERICA
Pacific Ocean
Atlantic Ocean

ASIA
MYANMAR
THAILAND
MALAYSIA
INDONESIA
Indian Ocean

THERE ARE FOUR SPECIES OF TAPIRS:
BAIRD'S, BRAZILIAN, MOUNTAIN, AND MALAYAN.

Threats to Wild Tapirs

- Illegal hunting, called poaching, for their meat and hide

- Loss of habitat, including land clearing for farming, cattle grazing, logging, urban areas, mining, and palm oil and rubber plantations

- Being killed by vehicles on roads that run through their habitat

- A low number of babies being born: females only have calves every two to three years

- Increased wildfires in tapir habitat because of climate change and human activities

Baird's

Brazilian

Mountain

Malayan

How You Can Help

To learn about conservation and how you can help the San Diego Zoo Wildlife Alliance save species worldwide, visit

support.sdzwa.org

Ten Things You and Your Family Can Do to Help Wildlife:

1. Learn about the local wildlife that lives in or near your community.

2. Create your own wildlife habitat by planting native bushes, flowers, and trees in your yard. You can put up a bird feeder, too.

3. Keep your cats indoors so they stay safe and don't hurt local wildlife, such as birds, lizards, and small mammals.

4. Tell your friends and family not to purchase products made from threatened trees and plants, marine organisms, or wild animals when traveling abroad.

5. Put trash that can't be recycled in a garbage can so it doesn't end up harming wildlife or traveling to the ocean.

6. Recycle paper products, glass bottles, cans, and plastic, and say "no" to plastic bottles, straws, lids, and cutlery.

7. Use a reusable water bottle.

8. Take your own reusable bags to the grocery store.

9. Volunteer to be a "citizen scientist" on **wildwatchkenya.org** and **wildwatchburrowingowl.org** to help researchers identify wildlife in photos taken by trail cameras (with your parents' permission).

10. Find out more about how climate change is affecting our planet and share this information with the people in your life.